PASSOVER
A Celebration of Freedom

By Bonnie Bader

Illustrated by Joanie Stone

A GOLDEN BOOK • NEW YORK

rhcbooks.com
Educators and librarians, for a variety of teaching tools, visit us at RHTeachersLibrarians.com
Library of Congress Control Number: 2021947511
ISBN 978-0-593-56388-5 (trade) — ISBN 978-0-593-56389-2 (ebook)
Printed in the United States of America
10 9 8 7 6 5 4 3 2 1

Tonight is a special holiday.
   The table is set, but it looks different
from all other nights. And we will eat food
that is different from all other nights. Why?
   Tonight we will gather to retell the story
of Passover. . . .

A long, long time ago, the Jewish people, called Israelites, lived in the land of Egypt. The Israelites were slaves, ruled by a powerful king called Pharaoh.

The slaves were forced to build the cities, palaces, and pyramids—brick by brick, day after day, under the hot sun, and with little food or water.
The Israelites cried out for their slavery to end.

God saw their pain and heard their cries and called on a man named Moses to lead the Israelites to freedom.

But Moses was an Egyptian. *Or was he?*

Moses grew up in Pharaoh's palace, but he was really born an Israelite.

As a baby, Moses's mother sent him down the Nile River. She wanted him to have a safer life than all the other Israelites in the land of Egypt.

Pharaoh's daughter found baby Moses in the water and decided to raise him as her own child.

Moses became a prince of Egypt. Yet when he saw the pain of the Israelites, his heart was filled with sadness. Deep down, he knew that the Israelites were his family.

One day, while Moses was out in the wilderness with his sheep, he saw a fiery bush. But strangely, the bush did not burn up.

Instead, a voice inside the bush told Moses that he would lead the Israelites to freedom. In that moment, Moses knew it was God who was talking. And Moses knew what he had to do.

Moses, along with his brother Aaron, went to Pharaoh and said, "Let my people go!"
But Pharaoh said no.
Moses told Pharaoh that if he didn't let the Israelites go, God would send bad things called plagues down to the people of Egypt. Pharaoh didn't listen. He didn't believe Moses.

So, as God instructed, Moses lifted up his staff and drove it into the waters of the Nile. The water in Egypt turned to blood.

But Pharaoh did not let the Israelites go.

Then God sent down frogs that hopped all over the land.

But Pharaoh did not let the Israelites go.

So God sent down more plagues:
Itchy lice jumped in and out of the Egyptians' hair.

Wild animals went into the
Egyptians' homes.
Cows and other livestock died.

Big sores bubbled up all
over the Egyptians' bodies.

Large hailstones fell from the sky.

A swarm of locusts swooped down
and ate all the crops.

All of Egypt was cast into darkness.

Then came the tenth plague—the worst plague
of all. Moses told Pharaoh that all the firstborn
children in Egypt would die.

But Pharaoh still did not let the Israelites go.

Moses told the Israelites to put lambs' blood on their doors. And when God saw the blood, he passed over the Israelites' homes. But the Egyptians' homes were not passed over, and the firstborn Egyptians died.

At last, Pharaoh agreed to let the Israelites go.

The Israelites were worried that Pharaoh would change his mind. They quickly packed everything they could carry. In their rush, they did not have enough time to let their bread rise. So they took the flat bread, called matzah, out of the oven and ran. . . .

Soon Pharaoh realized what he had done. "Who will build my cities?" he cried. Pharaoh commanded his army to stop the Israelites and bring them back.

The Israelites did not give up. They ran and ran until they reached the Red Sea. But the waters were deep, and they could not cross. They prayed to God for help.

God heard their prayers and parted the sea. The Israelites crossed on dry ground, with a wall of water on their left and a wall of water on their right. And as soon as they reached the other side, the sea closed up.

The Pharaoh's army could not follow them.

At last, the Israelites were free!

Tonight, we sit at our special table and eat special food during our Passover Seder. On the table is our Seder plate. We have a roasted bone, a roasted egg, parsley, bitter herbs, a mixture of sweet fruit and nuts called charoset, and some lettuce.

During the Seder, we sit comfortably and lean back on pillows. This reminds us that we are free and no longer slaves. We read from a special book called a Haggadah.

We dip parsley twice into salt water to remind us of the slaves' tears. We eat matzah to remember that the slaves didn't have time to let their bread rise. We eat charoset, which looks like the cement the slaves used to build the cities, but it tastes a whole lot better! And we eat bitter herbs to feel some of the slaves' bitterness.

After the meal, all the kids try to find the
hidden piece of matzah, called the afikomen.
But most important . . .

. . . tonight we retell the miraculous story of Passover.